AMERICA'S FUNNIEST MEMES:
Coronavirus Edition

Compiled by
Ed Mickolus

WANDERING
WOODS
PUBLISHERS

America's Funniest Memes: Coronavirus Edition

By Ed Mickolus

First Edition July 2020

ISBN: 978-1-949173-04-8

Published in the United States by
Wandering Woods Publishers

Book Design, Cover and Typesetting by
Cynthia J. Kwitchoff (CJKCREATIVE.COM)

Dedication

To all of the first responders and essential workers who
have put their lives on the line for all of us.

The Internet has been working overtime with humorous memes, tweets, Facebook postings, Pinterest collections, you name it during the pandemic crisis that as of this writing has killed 500,000 people, including 130,000 Americans. This outpouring of gallows humor suggests that we're coping with our profound grief and overcoming our fears, and we're going to eventually make it out of this, with our sense of humor, and self, intact. This book collects the best of funny, non-political memes from the COVID-19 era that translate well to verbal one-, two-, or several liners; there are hundreds of other sight gag memes that we'll save for another book. Some of the entries have been edited for language, spelling, and other typos. A big thank you goes out my favorite meme-finders, Brad Bouma, Maureen Wildey, Carol LaMothe, Rae Marzocchi and Kay Woodford; ace graphics arts designer Cynthia Kwitchoff; my wife and Blessing, Susan Schjelderup, who is getting the two of us through these trying times; and the hundreds of gifted albeit anonymous wits who wrote these memes.

Ed Mickolus
June 30, 2020

TABLE OF CONTENTS

Coronavirus Diary

Day 1 of quarantine: I'm going to take this as an opportunity to improve my health. Day Two: For personal reasons I am eating a lasagna in my shower.

Day 1 of Quarantine: Let's bake cookies. Day 14 of Quarantine: I think I ate too many cookies. Day 28 of Quarantine: I am a cookie.

Day 2 of Quarantine: The cats are plotting to kill me.

Day 3 and I'm already tired of babysitting my mom's grandkids.

Day 5 of social distancing: Had a conversation with a spider today. Seems nice. He's a web designer.

Quarantine Day 6: Went to this restaurant called The Kitchen. You have to gather all the ingredients and make your own meal. I have no clue how this place is still in business. @mommajessiec

Eight days into our family lockdown and I'm starting to question whether the Donner party was even hungry.

Quarantine Day 15: I walk around like everything is fine, but deep down, inside my shoe, my sock is sliding off.

Day 17: I've finished Netflix.

Also Day 17: Yesterday I wore something from 5 years ago and it actually fit! So proud of myself. It was a scarf. But still… Let's be positive here!

Day 19: I ordered a chicken and an egg from Amazon. I'll let you know.

Day 33: I've finished reading the Internet. Now what?

Day 40: Today I woke up, had a smoothie, and did an in-home workout. Translation: started drinking Margueritas at 10 a.m. and fell down the stairs.

There is a pandemic. We're gonna be in a future history class. We're gonna be remembered as the dumbest era of all time.

The longer this quarantine goes, the more I think Jack from The Shining actually held it together quite well.

Me: 2020 can't get any worse. News Item: Archeological team uncovers 6,000 year old chest buried deep in the Mediterranean Sea.

I'm not adding this year to my age. I didn't use it.

So far 2020 is like looking both ways before crossing the street and then getting hit by an airplane.

This is the first year I'm not going to Fiji because of Covid-19. I usually don't go because I'm poor.

Aliens probably fly past the Earth and lock their doors.

The world is now Vegas. Everybody's losing money, it's acceptable to drink at all hours, and no one has any idea what day it is.

Does anybody want to have a New Year's Eve party on June 30 and just pretend the first half was just a bad dream? I'll make margaritas.

I will admit that I did not have "monkey gang war" on my coronavirus bingo card.

Please don't mistake my humor about the virus as a lack of seriousness or concern. Laughing through hard times happens to be how I got through my whole life.

Apparently, referring to latex gloves as corona condoms at work is frowned upon.

Has anyone tried giving 2020 a Snickers?

Could someone enlighten me as to what the current crisis is that we are dealing with?

At this point, I wouldn't even be surprised if the dinosaurs returned.

What if aliens visited the Earth, while we were all on lockdown, and because nobody went to greet them they just went home again?

If 2020 were a drink, it would be a colonoscopy prep.

Kenny Rogers dippin' out in the middle of an apocalypse is the most "know when to fold 'em" thing ever.

Can not believe Tiger King was the most normal part of 2020.

2020: Written by Stephen King. Directed by Quentin Tarantino.

Computer, end program "2020" and delete the file.

Listen, guys. If June brings flying spiders, I'm out!

I can't believe it's riot season already. I still have my Covid-19 decorations up.

The virus must be really bad in India. I haven't gotten a call in days about my car's extended warranty.

After Tuesday, even the calendar goes W T F.

In 2020 we thought we'd have flying cars. But no, here we are teaching people how to wash their hands.

I think the term "shelter in place" came from up North. In the South we call it "hunker down". Just so we're all on the same page.

Today the devil whispered in my ear, "You're not strong enough to withstand the storm." And I whispered, "Six feet back, Lucifer!"

While y'all are trippin' over the coronavirus, I'm trying to figure out what the government is trying to cover up!

I'm getting pretty jealous of those 2 astronauts getting the hell off the planet…

March did Not come in like a lion. It came in like a T-Rex, with PMS, and hemorrhoids, wearing barbed wire undies.

Quarantine has given me the attention span of a goldfish.

People are mad about not being able to go places. Please. I was grounded about 90% of the time between 7th and 12th grade. I trained for this.

I'm having a quarantine party this weekend. None of you are invited.

I saw people through the window today. That's enough social interaction.

Home invasions should probably decline. Everyone is home with guns and enough bleach and paper towels to clean up the scene.

Mexico is now asking Trump to hurry up with the wall.

Can people stop trying to give me ideas on how to be productive during quarantine? Like I do my job and then watch Bravo for 5 hours and then go to bed like every other day. I'm not gonna organize my pantry, Brittany.

Has anyone tried unplugging 2020, waiting 10 seconds, and plugging it back in?

That "See you on Monday" turned into "See you in June" real quick.

Apparently one of the symptoms of Covid-19 is having no taste. Looking back on my exes I think I've been infected for years.

It's like we all complained about what a terrible year 2019 was and 2020 is like, 'here, hold my Corona."

To my parents who said staying home and playing video games would never prepare you for the real world: Checkmate.

I'm very disturbed by how many people seem to see washing their hands as a new thing.

If this were happening to the ancient Israelites we'd be stuck with an annual holiday where we'd have to stay inside for a month.

I can't believe I grew up for this.

Not to brag, but I haven't been late to anything in over two weeks.

Not to brag, but I've been avoiding people since way before the coronavirus.

Not to brag, but I was washing my hands before it became trending.

I'm not ready to die. I haven't gotten to wear a fur coat and tell a man I don't love him back yet.

My 90 day trial of 2020 is up. I would like to unsubscribe.

I'd like to cancel my 3 month trial of 2020. Not impressed. Do not recommend.

I'm sorry for what I said when we were quarantined.

With March and April basically canceled, the next holiday is... wait for it... Cinco de Mayo, sponsored by Corona.

Adding "showed up to work during the coronavirus" to my resume.

I think I'm finally being grounded for everything I wasn't caught for as a teenager.

I don't like that my chances of survival seem to be linked to the common sense of others.

2020 came out all looking like a warm chocolate chip cookie. Then one bite and bam. Oatmeal raisin.

Turns out my top 3 hobbies are:

- Eating at restaurants
- Going to nonessential businesses
- Touching my face

Until further notice, the days of the week are now called Thisday, Thatday, Otherday, Someday, Yesterday, Today, and Nextday.

Household log entry: Wine supply depleted. Candy dwindling.   Must don real clothes and exit base. Human interaction likely. Morale low. Prognosis grim.

After being quarantined for weeks and someone asks me if I'm a morning person, or a night person, I'm like: I honestly don't know anymore.

I wish corona could've started in Las Vegas because what happens in Vegas stays in Vegas.

I'm so excited it's time to take the garbage out. I wonder what I should wear?

I need about 50 people to join me so that we can dress up as Zombies and walk around the neighborhood. Can't let this quarantine go to waste.

Somebody tell Pollen to hold up. We are trying to deal with Rona right now. One problem at a time.

Mom always told me I wouldn't amount to anything lying on the sofa. And yet here I am, saving the world!

Grocery shopping has become a real-life version of Pac-Man. Avoid everyone, get the fruit, and take any route to avoid contact.

When does Season 2 of 2020 start? I do not like Season 1!

I collect all cell phones and iPads from the kids at night and keep them in my room. Last night they all set alarms to go off at various times throughout the night. I'm impressed with their ingenuity and team effort. They're all grounded.

People who are quarantining in jeans: what are you trying to prove?

Finally shaved my legs and donated it to Locks of Love.

It could be worse. The Internet could go down.

People are panicking and always trading sex for food. It's crazy. Anyways, I got a Klondike bar.

I am a creature of habit. Being locked inside 24/7 was not one of those habits. Who even am I now?

Has anybody let the Amish know what's going on yet?

Quarantine life: I don't know who needs to hear this, but today is Saturday.

Bet y'all stop walking around eating grapes at Walmart now.

What a great time to be alive. It's like the great plague, but with wifi.

Some of y'all went from DIY homemade, natural, all organic cleaning product to Clorox real fast.

If you're happy and you know it, stay in bed. If you're happy and you know it, stay in bed. If you're happy and you know it, getting up will surely blow it. If you're happy and you know it, stay in bed.

If you want the South to take this coronavirus seriously, you have to have Jim Cantore report it live from a beach.

Was stuck in line, 6 deep at Publix. So after I coughed I said, "This cough is getting worse since I got back from China." Boom, no line!

The weekend: 80 degrees, a holiday, and the stay at home order lifted. Translation: people are about to act up and we'll be grounded by Wednesday.

To be honest, I have wanted to spray a lot of people with Lysol before all this started.

On the tenth day of quarantine, my true life gave to me:

- 10 days a-drinking
- 9 veggies wasted
- 8 days-a-lounging
- 7 Uber eats
- 6 daily meals
- 5 Panic Attacks!
- 4 new fears
- 3 a.m. bedtime
- 2 bug friends

- And a chin that wasn't there before!

April Fool's Day has been canceled this year because no made up prank could ever compare to the unbelievable stuff happening right now in the world.

Curious — does anyone happen to know when we find out which Hunger Games district we are in?

Sometimes I wonder if all this is happening because I didn't forward that email to 10 people.

Everything for the summer is canceled. May as well just put up the Christmas tree and call it a year!

Imagine if this lockdown happened 18 years ago. You would be stuck at home with a Nokia 3310 with 300 texts, 100 minutes call limit and dialup Internet.

I got pulled over in the HOV lane for driving alone. I said that due to social distancing, my passenger was in the car behind me.

So, in retrospect, in 2015, not a single person got the answer right to "where do you see yourself five years from now?"

It turns out I was social distancing the whole time.

I know everything happens for a reason, but WTF.

I never thought in my entire life my hands would consume more alcohol than my mouth.

I've been waiting for the perfect time to change my Netflix password so my ex can't use it anymore and it really doesn't get any better than a national lockdown.

In an unsettling reversal of my teenage years, I am now yelling at my parents for going out.

Our cleaning lady just called and told us she will be working from home and will send us instructions on what to do.

This is the biggest game of cooties I've ever seen in my life.

Of all the things I learned in grade school, trying to avoid cooties was the last one I expected to use.

What a year this week has been.

The longer this goes on the harder it will be to return to a society where pants and bras are required.

Pigeons probably think we're extinct.

Apparently this year is being written by Stephen King.

Would y'all please keep your butts at home? I have stuff to do this summer!

Roses are red. April is gray. I pray we can all leave our houses in May.

This virus has done what no woman had been able to do... cancel all sports, shut down all bars, and keep men at home!

Now that we have everyone washing their hands correctly, next week: Turn Signals!

Wow. Bars, gyms and clubs all closed? My life is about to be seriously exactly the same.

Can y'all just follow the government instructions so we can knock this COVID-19 out and be done? I feel like a kindergartener that keeps losing more recess time because one or two kids can't follow directions.

Me posting nonsense will continue during lockdown because it's an essential service.

I went outside and felt something wet on my arm. It was a mosquito using a wet wipe before it bit me.

What if this quarantine is just the aliens fattening us up before the big harvest?

I never thought the comment "I'd never touch him/her with a 6-foot pole" would become a national policy, but here we are.

I'm getting tired of being part of a major historical event.

I'm not counting this year towards my age.

2020 is the strictest parent I've ever had.

If they had just called it the "Stay at Home Challenge" and posted it on Facebook, the virus would be gone by now.

Don't know why my fishing buddy is worried about catching the coronavirus. He never catches anything.

After years of wanting to thoroughly clean the house but lacking the time, this week I discovered that wasn't the reason.

This week I am going to sling some candy out the door, toss a turkey in the oven, open a few presents, and call it a year.

2020 is what happens when you mix up cards from your tarot deck and Cards Against Humanity.

COPING: Some Good, Some Maybe Not the Best Coping Mechanisms

I practiced social distancing by playing golf. There is never anyone around where I hit the ball. FORE!

To all the people who are panic buying, make sure you stock up on condoms, so you don't produce any more idiots.

Nobody: So how much money y'all spent on Amazon since quarantine? Me: What happens on Amazon Prime, Stays on Amazon Prime.

Come to the dark side. We have masks and respirators.

(Photo of King Tut's coffin) Put him back!

Scene: A crowded beach. Mummy, am I going to school tomorrow? No, son; it's not safe.

Dear Lord, Please don't let Brussels Sprouts be a part of the cure for Covid-19 virus.

Can somebody pull 2020 out of the Nintendo and blow on the cartridge? It ain't playing right.

The man on the news said at the end of the day, what's going to keep you safe is common sense. Some of y'all in trouble.

List of things I'm handling well currently:

> 1.

I washed my hands so much, my exam notes from 1995 re-surfaced.

Can't spell Pandemic without Panic.

Today's Forecast: Lazy with a 90% chance of Netflix.

Corona email sign-offs:
- Quarantined regards,
- Yours from afar,
- Cautious cheers,
- Best (but could be better),
- Socially distant,
- Take care — no but really,
- In no haste,
- Sent from my living room,
- Until three weeks,

Government: Only go outside for emergencies. People's emergencies: I wanted iced coffee!

Breaking: Due to the coronavirus, all gym-related activities have been suspended indefinitely. My summer body has been postponed until 2021. Thank you for your patience.

Note in refrigerator: Please remember to date the food cans! Thanks. Second note: Tried on three occasions to date cans. They only think of me as a friend.

Coronavirus: Everybody stay inside. Earthquake: Everybody run outside. God: You put the scared people in. You put the scared people out, and you shake them all about.

#notmyvirus That should do the trick!

- Monday: No gatherings > 500 people
- Tuesday: No gatherings > 50 people
- Wednesday: No gatherings > 10 people
- Thursday: Stay 6 feet away from people.
- Friday: Stay home.
- Tomorrow: OK, floor is lava.

And just like that I went from fabric hoarding to being prepared.

I'm no scientist, but has anyone tried killing coronavirus with the bowling alley shoe spray yet?

Self Isolation Presents: Stay at Home Music Festival March 2020, featuring

- Couch Test Dummies
- The Coughspring
- The Indoors
- Pandemic at the Disco
- No Kids on the Block
- Flu Fighters
- No Cure
- Miley Virus
- Men Out of Work
- Depressed Mode
- Billy Idle

- Wu-Han Clan
- Pearl Jammies
- Special Guest: System of a Lockdown

Keep calm and wash your hands.

HR explaining to me that I can't be yelling "This %^&* Got the Rona" at every co-worker who coughs.

Dear extraverts: You will survive this. Dear introverts: Quit laughing! They're new to this social distancing.

I have very high expectations for all of you. When Shakespeare was quarantined because of the plague, he wrote King Lear.

Officer, I wasn't speeding! It's called social distancing and you were following too close.

With so many sporting events cancelled, they're going to televise the World Origami Championship. It's on Paper-view.

At least now we know who our state's governor is.

Sign: Covid testing in the rear Me: And I thought it was a nasal swab!

Kill germs the Cajun Way: Tabasco. Not only does it kill germs, it also prevents you from sticking your fingers in your eyes, nose, and mouth (and other places) a second time.

Having trouble forcing yourself to stay home? Shave your eyebrows off.

I just Clorox wiped a bottle of Purell and Purelled my hands because I touched the Clorox canister. How far down a rabbit hole does this go?

Five creative reframes in a time of COVID-19:

Shelter-in-place	Artist-in-residence
Quarantine out of fear of self-protection	Quarantine out of concern for collective well-being
Social distancing	Physical distancing
Isolation and loneliness	Solidarity in solitude
Economic collapse	Ecological renewal

For those who have lost track, today is Blursday the forthteenth of Maprilay.

My body has absorbed so much soap and water, hand sanitizer and disinfectant that now when I pee, it cleans the toilet.

30 days hath September, April, June and November. All the rest have 31, except March, which has 1,549 days.

If the past few weeks have taught us anything, it's that stupidity spreads faster than any virus ever could.

I swear we are fighting two pandemics: coronavirus and stupidity!

Alert: DUI checkpoint at the corner of Kitchen and Hallway.

Hugh Hefner became a multimillionaire by staying home in his jammies. I'm not having the same result.

Spain canceled the Running of the Bulls. Germany canceled Octoberfest. Georgia opened the massage parlors.

We need to change who is in charge of this crisis. Three phone calls, Radar could've had masks, gloves, ventilators, PPE, 12-year-old Scotch, Rocky Road ice cream and grape-flavored Nehi soda.

Some people only write lockdown because they can't spell kwarinteen.

Whatever song was #1 on your 12th birthday is your quarantine theme song.

Anyone who is acting like buying hand sanitizer and soap is new, remember who they are and don't eat their cooking.

I can't wait until this is over, so I can go back to social distancing on my own terms!

Remember when we were little and had underwear with the days of the week on them? Yah. Those would be helpful right now.

Gwenyth Paltrow said in an interview we should take this time to learn a new language or write a book. I just shook chip crumbs out of my bra and have no idea what day it is. I'm fairly certain I'm not going to attempt either of those things.

Quarantine has turned all of us into dogs. We roam the house all day looking for food. We are told "no" if we get too close to strangers. And we get really excited about car rides.

And just like that: having a mask, rubber gloves, duct tape, plastic sheeting and a rope in your trunk is ok.

Did a load of pajamas so I would have clean work clothes this week.

Six easy exercises while in quarantine:

- Trying to get up from the couch
- Staggering to bed drunk
- Staring into the fridge
- Checking if your feet are still there
- Covering your ears to make the voices stop
- Abandoning all hopes and dreams

Every time I feel a tickle in my throat: Is that you, Rona?

Remember before you go out and do something stupid… we have no idea when you'll be able to see the judge.

"I can't go out because of coronavirus" — whiny, boring, weak. "I've sworn an oath of solitude until the blight is purged from these lands." –heroic, valiant. They will assume you have a sword. Impossible to check if you really have a sword because of coronavirus.

Oh, noowww everyone wants to know what introverts do for fun…

In light of new social distancing ordinances, banjo players shall be posted on every street corner to discourage public gatherings.

Prisoner 1: What you in for? Prisoner 2: I was in Publix and walked the wrong direction down the grocery aisle.

Due to the quarantine I'll only be telling inside jokes.

Coronavirus tip: Wear a Jaguars jersey and you won't catch anything.

Tee-shirt message of the week: I didn't see anyone today so I'm wearing this again tomorrow.

Due to coronavirus I will not shake hands or hug... you may kneel or bow to me... either will be fine.

50 Ways to Beat This Virus:

- Stay away from the pack, Jack
- Don't visit your Gran, Stan
- Wipe down every toy, Roy
- To keep virus-free
- Don't hop on the bus, Gus
- Don't listen to Don, Ron
- Don't hoard the TP, Lee
- Just stay virus free
- Sneeze into your sleeve, Steve
- Stop touching your face, Grace
- Keep back to six feet, Pete
- Heed the CDC
- Just use the Purell, Mel
- Keep wipes in your purse, Nurse
- Take care of your stock, Doc
- You need PPE
- This isn't Spring Break, Jake
- Stop home if you're sick, Dick
- As COVID leaps, peeps
- Just follow the rules, fools
- And stay virus-free

Hobby Eating

I never would have believed that a few weeks of uncut hair would weigh 20 pounds but that's what the scale says.

If you haven't seen me in a while, I'm fat now. You don't have to tell me. Thanks in advance.

So what you are telling me is that the coronavirus made you eat all day?

It's gardening season: 5 weeks ago I planted myself on the sofa and I've grown considerably.

Public service announcement: Every few days, try on your jeans to see if they still fit. Pajamas will have you believe all is well in the kingdom.

Breaking news: Wearing a mask inside your home is now highly recommended. Not so much to prevent COVID-19 but to stop eating.

We are not frightened enough to eat tofu yet.

Due to coronavirus, my summer body will be delayed until 2021. Thanks for understanding.

I swear my refrigerator just said, "What? You again?"

After all the eating I've done, I'm happy to report my flip-flops still fit.

My Disney Princess name is Taco Belle.

I need to Social Distance from the kitchen. I tested positive for a big butt.

Now that the gyms are closed, this summer gonna be about personality.

Not sure what's scarier at this point: taking my temperature or weighing myself.

On average, the Panda feeds for 15 hours a day. This is the same as an adult at home under quarantine, which is why we call it a "Pandemic".

Pretty wild how we used to eat cake after someone had blown on it... Good times...

Germany is now advising people to stock up on cheese and sausages. This is called the Wurst Kase scenario.

New monthly budget:
- Gas $0
- Entertainment $0
- Clothes $0
- Groceries $1624

I may act like I'm ok, but deep down inside... I'm hungry again.

Restaurants are closed. I hope y'all picked someone who can cook.

Good morning, self-isolation inmates! Anyone know how much vodka goes in scrambled eggs?

How to stop eating during quarantine. Wear your swimsuit instead of your pajamas. You're welcome.

Clean eating: Having breakfast after you've showered.

Fight coronavirus! Eat five cloves of garlic every day. It does absolutely nothing, but keeps everyone at a safe distance.

Wanted: someone to hand feed me Doritos so my fingers don't get orange. No weirdos.

Hormel made their first batch of Spam in 1937. The company just announced that due to hoarding by customers, they are going to make a second batch.

Anyone want to meet for lunch tomorrow? We could order drive-through and pull up next to each other like the cops do.

The buttons on my jeans have started social distancing from each other.

Anyone else starting to get a tan from the light in the fridge?

Now that I've lived during a plague, I understand why most Renaissance paintings are of chubby women laying around without a bra.

Stepped on my scale this morning and it said: Please use social distancing; one person at a time.

Had I known in March that it was the last time I would be in a restaurant, I would have ordered the dessert.

Whoa, this is a lot of days in a row to have to make dinner.

When swimsuit season hits, I want y'all to remember that the gyms were closed during Reese's Peanut Butter Eggs season.

I've eaten 14 meals and taken 6 naps and it's still today. Are you kidding me?

I need to find hobbies that don't include eating or buying things.

At first, I thought I had Covid because I couldn't breathe. Then I unbuttoned my pants and it was all ok.

What if they close the grocery stores? We'll have to hunt for food. I don't even know where Doritos live.

My grocery list: 1. Don't run into anyone I know. 2. Eggs.

How y'all summer body lookin'? Mine lookin' like I have a great personality.

Does anybody else feel like they've cooked 450 dinners this month?

Dear Netflix: Can you please turn off the "are you still watching" feature? We are in quarantine so yes we are still watching. I don't need this kind of judgment in this time of uncertainty. If you could please update it with a "are you sure you want to eat that" notice that would be much more helpful at this time. *Sincerely, Me*

I've gained so much weight in isolation that the last time I went for a walk I showed up on Google Maps as a round-about.

Hobby Drinking

Jack Daniels: Anti-corona virus spray. Spray throat three times a day.

Keep in mind, even during a pandemic, no matter how much chocolate you eat or beer you drink, your earrings will still fit.

The worst thing about returning to bars will be getting a standard 5-ounce pour of wine instead of the 25-ounces my home-bar offers.

Happy hour is starting earlier and earlier. If this keeps up, I'll be pouring wine in my cereal.

How come the liquor stores don't have empty shelves? Are people not realizing they will be quarantined with their spouses and kids?

Quarantini: just a regular martini, but you drink it all alone in your house.

Bingeing while cringing.

I'm either coming out of this quarantine 20 pounds lighter, chakras balanced and a house full of complete craft projects, or… 20 pounds heavier with a drinking problem.

2020 has no rules. Care to join me for a glass of breakfast wine?

Home Isolation has its ups and downs. One day you're flying high and cleaning the baseboards with a Q-Tip, and the next day you're drinking tequila and watching squirrels out the window. There's no in between.

For the third time this week I'm buying booze for the next two weeks.

Just to be clear, we've all agreed that liquor stores are "essential" and schools are not!

Moonshine? No, officer, we're making hand sanitizer.

Just tried making hand sanitizer, but it came out as jello shots.

How crazy is this: I just tried to make my own hand sanitizer, and it came out as a rum and Coke.

Is it OK to pull the bag of wine out of the box and stab it with a straw like it's a giant adult Capri Sun? Asking for a friend.

Don't know how I feel about bars opening back up. Drinks gonna be weak compared to what I've been pouring.

(photo of packed stadium): Alcoholics Anonymous 2021

If you keep a glass of wine in each hand you can't accidentally touch your face.

First it was: alcohol kills Covid. Then heat may kill Covid. Now direct sunlight may kill Covid. So if you see me outside in my yard drunk, naked, and laying in the sun, mind your own business. I'm conducting important medical experiments.

Covid-19 got us all like: Karen! Come look at all the wine bottles in Linda's recycling bin!

You're not allowed to visit me. But you can leave liquor on the porch.

Travel – Not!

Now I understand why Laura Ingalls would get so excited when she'd get to go into town with Pa.

Telling your luggage there will be no vacation this year can be tough. Emotional baggage is the worst.

My shoes probably think I died.

Travel plans this week: To the window, to the wall, might go down the hall…

And just like that my car is getting 3 weeks to the gallon.

Me: Alexa, what's the weather going to be like this week? Alexa: Why? Where do you think you're going?

Alexa, what's the weather supposed to be like tomorrow? Alexa: Don't worry about it. You ain't going anywhere.

Weekend Travel Plans:
- To the window
- To the wall
- Then I might skip down the hall

New Airport Codes for our Current Travels:

- LVG Living Room
- DNG Dining Room
- BTH Bathroom
- BKY Back yard
- PAT Patio
- MBR Master Bedroom
- OFC Office
- WNC Wine Cellar

Your Horoscope this week:

- Aries: You'll be spending time in your home.
- Taurus: You'll be spending time in your home.
- Gemini: You'll be spending time in your home.
- Cancer: You'll be spending time in your home.
- Leo: You'll be spending time in your home.
- Virgo: You'll be spending time in your home.
- Libra: You'll be spending time in your home.
- Scorpio: You'll be spending time in your home.
- Sagittarius: You'll be spending time in your home.
- Capricorn: You'll be spending time in your home.
- Aquarius: You'll be spending time in your home.
- Pisces: You'll be spending time in your home.

It's like being 16 again. Gas is cheap and I'm grounded.

We can save the world if we just stay at home lying on the sofa watching TV. Let's not mess this up.

Remember going places? That was awesome.

I hope the weather is good tomorrow for my trip to Puerto Backyarda. I'm getting tired of Los Livingroom.

Gas prices at an all-time low, but nowhere to go.

I'm a homebody but dang I did like going to one or two places.

Where is your next travel destination:
- Las Kitchenas
- Los Lounges
- Santa Bedroomes
- Porto Gardenas
- Los Bed
- Costa del Balconia
- St. Bathroom
- La Rotonda de Sofa

Boredom

I have come to the conclusion that buying craft supplies and actually using them are two separate hobbies.

Can't wait until tomorrow. I have another big day of hand washing and looking out the window planned.

I know you're bored, but do Not cut your own bangs.

I promised myself I'd do things differently tonight. So I'm sitting at the other end of the couch.

Everything is cancelled. You know what is not cancelled? Laundry. Laundry is never cancelled.

The Associated Press reported that "South African Breweries… may have to destroy 400 million bottles of beer." That's going to be a really long song. Let's get started: "400 million bottles of beer on the wall…"

It is not boring at all to stay in the house. But how come a bag of rice has 7,456 pieces and the other bag 7,398?

Is it too soon to put up the Christmas tree yet? I've run out of things to do.

Starting to understand why pets try to run out of the house when the front door opens.

I don't mean to brag, but... I just put together a puzzle in 1 day and the box said 2-4 years.

Apparently it's Saturday.

Think you're bored? Sir Isaac Newton invented Calculus during the plague. Do you have any idea how bored you must be to invent Calculus?

I was so bored last night I called Jake from State Farm just to talk to somebody. (He asked me what I was wearing.)

What are you wearing, Jake from State Farm? Um, a Hazmat suit.

The dumbest thing I've ever purchased was a 2020 planner.

Our Pets Speak Out

My dog is looking at me like, "See, this is why I chew the furniture."

Dog: Please don't walk me again. Find something to watch on Netflix. Read a book. But leave me alone!

Dog: Looking to rehome my humans. They are now here 24/7 and I can't catch a wink of my daytime sleep. Going for walks multiple times a day! Curtailing my squirrel and possum stalking. They be stinking up the house with bleach and just won't let me bark at the UPS man. Free to good home.

You thought dogs were hard to train? Look at all the humans who can't sit and stay.

Cat: Why are the annoying servants staying in my home all day now?

Dog on top of refrigerator: No, I'm Not coming down. We've been on 20 walks today. Leave me alone.

What are you doing, human? Working? Can I help? I want to help. I could sit on your keyboard for you!

All of our dogs think we quit our jobs to spend more time with them. All of our cats think we got fired for being the loser they always knew we were.

Practicing social distancing and cleaning yourself? Congratulations, my friend, you've become a house cat.

After listening to her owner drone on for hours, Ginger suddenly realized she was Not cut out to be an emotional support dog after all.

My first instinct when I see an animal is to say "hello". My first instinct when I see a person is to avoid eye contact and hope it goes away.

Squirrel looking miffed: Covid this. Covid that. The bird feeder's still empty, Karen. It wouldn't kill you to fill it.

Dog: All the humans with muzzles! Who did they bite?

Dogs: What's happening? Why are all the humans wearing muzzles?

The World Health Organization has announced that dogs cannot contract COVID-19. Dogs previously held in quarantine can be released. To be clear: WHO let the dogs out.

Who Needs The Hunt for Red October When We've Got The Hunt for Toilet Paper?

Neighbor's house got TPd last night. Now it's listed on Zillow for $12.5 million.

Grandpa, tell us a story about the olden days. Back before the great TP war of 2020, we had so much TP we used to hang it off the houses and trees of our enemies.

Some people aren't shaking hands because of the coronavirus. I'm not shaking hands because everyone is out of TP.

The panic, market crash, and TP hoarding over COVID-19 is a good indicator of why the public can never be told what's really going on in Area 51.

Dear Girl: I may run out of TP, but I will never run out of love for you.

Until further notice: No one can stop by unannounced. We aren't sick, we just don't trust you with our TP.

No idea what wiped the Earthlings out...but they had the cleanest butts I've ever seen.

I asked a Walmart worker where I could find the nuts. He said they're in the toilet paper aisle.

Due to toilet paper shortage, please use the litter box until further notice.

Single man with Purell and Lysol seeking single woman with toilet paper for some good, clean fun.

Seeing all the jokes about toilet paper shortages:

- I don't find them very Charmin.
- It's Scott to stop soon.
- This is Northern to laugh about!
- Is this some kind of vast 2-ply conspiracy? Very hard to absorb it all.
- I mean, it wipes me out!
- I guess I will just roll along with everyone else.
- I have to go now… I'm feeling flushed.

I still can't believe people's survival instincts told them to grab toilet paper.

I just read on the interweb that murder hornets can spread COVID-19 telepathically over the 5G network. Can anyone confirm? I think I'm going to need more toilet paper.

Don't hoard the left hand or the toilet paper!

Since everyone has lost their minds and hoarded all the toilet paper, mind ya business when you see me scooting across the lawn. You created this monster.

I have a 24-pack of toilet paper (2-ply!). Looking to trade for a 4 BR house.

Border police have just seized 2 tons of toilet paper hidden in cocaine.

If a diarrhea virus hit us right now, do you think people would buy up all the nasal spray?

99 rolls of toilet paper on the wall, 99 rolls… We know who you are!

You've heard of Panic! At the Disco. Get ready for Panic! at the Costco.

We are out of toilet paper. More coming on 3/01/25020. Sorry for the inconvenience.

If you need 144 rolls of toilet paper for a 14-day quarantine, you probably should've been seeing a doctor long before COVID-19.

I just got gas for $1.47. I'm not telling you guys where. 'Cause I see how y'all did the toilet paper.

You never appreciate what you have till it's gone. Toilet paper is a good example.

In the future, my grandchildren may ask about the global crisis of 2020 and how the world was tragically out of TP. I plan to tell them that we had to drag our butts across the grass. Up hill both ways. In the snow.

Young people have had to go from trying to find someone over 21 to buy them alcohol to finding someone over 60 to buy them toilet paper.

And in the end mankind used so much TP they wiped themselves out.

So I said to Arnold, "Where'd you get all the TP?" He said, "Aisle B, back."

Due to panic buying, Walmart has opened register number 3.

Want to find out who your real friends are? Ask to borrow a roll of toilet paper.

Doctor: Your COVID-19 test came back positive. Patient: That can't be correct. I have more than 300 rolls of toilet paper.

I used to spin that toilet paper roll like I was on the Wheel of Fortune. Now I turn it like I'm cracking a safe.

Back in my day, the only time we started panic buying was when the bartender yelled "last call".

Photo of empty TP roll on which is written: What Would McGiver Do?

My son spotted the empty TP shelves and asked, does this mean everyone will start wearing pull-ups? I said, "depends"…

Does anyone know how long toilet paper lasts if you freeze it?

Ran out of toilet paper and now using lettuce leaves. Today was just the tip of the iceberg, tomorrow romaines to be seen.

(Photo of log) Raw toilet paper for sale $20. Some assembly required.

I see a gap in your resume for 2020; what were you doing then? Looking for toilet paper.

It was a quiet Monday morning in September 2053, when John awoke with a need to go to the bathroom. To John this wasn't just any ordinary day! This was the day he would open the last package of toilet paper his parents bought in the year 2020.

In 20 years when kids ask about the 2020 toilet paper shortage, I'm telling them we had to drag our butts across the lawn. In the snow. Uphill. Both ways. Dodging murder hornets.

Grooming

Pro tip: You should wash your hands even when there isn't a global virus panic.

Dear the people who are buying 30 bottles of hand soap leaving the supermarket shelves bare, you do realize to stop the spread of a virus you need other people to wash their hands, too?

Salons have been closed for so long that there are no more selfies. Everyone is now making avatars!

Does anyone know if we can take showers yet or do we just keep washing our hands?

Have y'all noticed that since beauty salons are closed selfies are down 68%?

Fact: In four weeks, 88% of blonds will disappear from the earth.

Reminder: 9 p.m. is the time to remove your day pajamas and put your night pajamas on.

Nail salons-closed. Hair salons-closed. Lash salons-closed. It's about to get real ugly out here.

Day 41: I'm one more missed haircut away from buying Aquanet and an 1800-watt blow dryer and cranking my hair up to 1986.

Do not call the police about suspicious people in your neighborhood. These are your neighbors without hair coloring, make up, and hair extensions.

Feels like we're 3-4 weeks away from learning everyone's real hair color.

Just because you haven't gone anywhere all day doesn't mean you don't have to take a bath.

During this time, I'm thankful to be low maintenance. No nails to fix, no eye lashes to maintain, no care in the world about roots. I knew being a hot mess would pay off some day!

People are asking who is still doing nails and hair… Your local mortician. Stay home!

Guess who is open to do your hair, nails, and eyebrows? The funeral home! If you want an appointment, keep running around.

Homeschooling

Parents who tell teachers how to do their jobs, This is your moment to shine!

I see all you parents aren't excited about your kids' first day of school. Not one dang first day picture!

I wonder how those "I'll never spank my children" parents are doing. Y'all good?

It may take a village to raise a child, but I swear it's gonna take a vineyard to homeschool one!

Being a teacher is easy. It's like riding a bike. Except the bike is on fire. You're on fire. Everything is on fire. And you're in Hell.

Homeschooling Day 3: They all graduated yesterday.

Homeschooling Day 5: For science class we studied the effects of Nyquil on students.

Teacher: So what did we learn during quarantine, kids?

- Dad is not smarter than a fifth grader.
- Mum can drink Dad under the table.
- China sucks!
- You don't need toilet paper to wipe your butt!

Quarantine Day One: This could be fun! I've always wondered what it would be like to homeschool! Quarantine Day One [at breakfast]: SO HELP ME GOD, MOVE YOUR FOOT AWAY FROM YOUR BROTHER'S CEREAL BOWL OR I WILL FIND A SCHOOL IN THIS COUNTRY THAT IS OPEN AND DRIVE US THERE TODAY.

Homeschool Diary, Day 1: Wondering how I can get this kid transferred out of my class.

Homeschool Diary, Day 2: Need a sub.

Homeschool Diary, Day 3: Helped my 6-year-old with telling the time. For instance, how there are 60 seconds in a minute, 60 minutes in an hour, and 245,934,992 hours in 2 days of homeschooling.

Homeschool Diary, Day 4: Today there was a lot of yelling and crying, things were thrown around, it was anarchy. But I calmed down and apologized to the kids and they seem ok about it.

Homeschool Diary, Day 5: My child just said "I hope I don't have the same teacher next year."

Homeschool Diary, Day 6: Johnny telephoned from upstairs to say he would not be in school as he missed the bus.

Homeschool Diary, Day 7: My 6-year-old said she was really missing her teacher. She said it TO MY FACE. A bit rude.

Homeschool Diary, Day 9: Today we did math. If you have 3 kids, and they are awake roughly 13 hours in the day, and you're trying to work from home, home many times will you hear the word "snack"?

Homeschool Diary, Day 12: Fed the math homework to the dog myself.

Homeschooling going well: Two students suspended for fighting and one teacher fired for drinking on the job.

Dad, the lunch lady said some really bad words today. Son, your mother is under a lot of stress these days.

Homeschool Day 1 with Dad: Passed oil changing.

Schools: We're shutting down. Keep your kids at home. Parents: Keep them in my house? Where I live?

You can either have a nice day or you can help your child with their math homework. You can't have both. –Coronalations 03:30

Home schooling question: Does having your children fix you mixed cocktails count as Chemistry? (Sorry, I'm new at this.)

When do we usually find out who the kids will have as teachers next year? I hope it's not me again…

OK, the schools are closed. So do we drop the kids off at the teacher's house, or what?

History essays in 2053: Explain the use and role of memes as a coping mechanism during the Corona Virus Pandemic of 2020.

She: The teacher inside doesn't know anything about math. She makes me want to drink. He: Stop it, Carole! Mom is trying.

Tomorrow is the National Homeschool Tornado Drill. Lock your kids in the basement until you give the all clear. You're welcome.

Parents are homeschooling today like: "If you got eight… #$%^&… apples…"

All these kids been learning Common Core Math 'bout to learn "carry the one" from their new homeschool teachers.

I am a horrible homeschool teacher. My child has been at recess since 9:30 a.m.

Study finds that parents can do ⅓ of their kids' maths, but struggle with the other ¾.

Quarantine parenting. The struggle is real. Dad to daughter: Please go play with your brother. That's basically the reason we had him.

Parents across the country: Our children will be home from school for weeks; what are we going to do? Homeschool Parents: Welcome to the jungle!

Does anyone know that parent we are supposed to call if we need a substitute teacher?

You lied. My kids are not a joy to have in class!

School closing over COVID-19. Homeschool moms everywhere: We've trained for this!

2019 homeschooled population: 3.4% 2020 homeschooled population: 100% Scheesh! Everyone wants to be a hipster!

Normal parents: Schools are closed! Math! Latin verbs! OMG! Homeschoolers: Hold my beer.

I finally had "the talk" with my kids. I told them how some animals eat their young. So they better get their stuff together before dinner.

If you see my kid on Zoom in the same clothes he's been wearing the past five days, mind your business . . . our homeschool has a uniform.

Gonna ask my Mom if that offer to slap me into the next year is still on the table.

Somewhere out there there's a kid who brought home the class hamster for the weekend. The parents are not happy!

Saw my neighbor Tammy out early this morning scraping the "My kid is a terrific student" sticker off her minivan. Guess that first week of homeschooling didn't go so well.

Wondering how many students are missing their old teachers because their new one is mean.

Three weeks of home schooling my 7, 9, and 12-year olds went surprisingly well! They have all graduated from High School and are now ready to move out and get jobs when the quarantine is lifted.

I'm done with homeschooling. We are switching to trade school. Mine are going to be bartenders.

And just like that, no one ever asked a stay-at-home mom what she does all day ever again.

I will teach you in a room. I will teach you now on Zoom. I will teach you in a house. I will teach you with my mouse. I will teach you here or there. I will teach you because I care.

This homeschool thing wouldn't be so bad if we had a better janitor.

Just asked a 6-year-old if he understands why there is no school. He said yes, because they are out of toilet paper.

If you see my kids crying outside and picking weeds, just keep driving. They're on a field trip.

Dear Parents: Tag, you're it. –Love, Teachers

Dear Parents: Don't worry. Teaching gets easier. The first 5 years are always the hardest.

Dear public school moms: We can't wait until your kids are back in school, either! Signed, Homeschool moms everywhere

Alexa: Homeschool the children!

And just like that, spankings and prayer is back in school.

Some of you parents are about to find out: the teacher wasn't the problem.

Don't have any kids at home anymore, so I tried to homeschool my husband. It didn't work. He's in detention.

Not everyone knows this but a homeschool day is actually 40 times as long as a regular day.

Two weeks into homeschool and my 9 year old has already broken the world record for longest amount of time spent sharpening a pencil.

[Homeschool field trip to the laundry room] Kids: Dad, what IS this place? Dad: I have absolutely no idea.

OK teachers. Well played. We'll give you the raises and the respect you deserve. Now give us the antidote and take our kids back.

Does anyone know the number parents are supposed to call if we need a substitute teacher?

The best thing about homeschooling is that now I can add "I'll fail you" to my repertoire of empty parenting threats.

Teachers: still think they're overpaid?

Teachers: Name your price. We're listening.

My neighbor just yelled at her kid so loud that even I brushed my teeth and went to bed.

If there's one thing that scares me more than an apocalyptic end to the world, it's the possibility that if my kids fail at homeschooling they have to retake it.

First day of homeschool and my 13-year-old tried to call in sick…

If you see my boys locked outside, mind your business. We're having a fire drill.

If you see me talking to myself this week, mind your business. I'm having a parent-teacher conference.

Have you considered in-home suspension? Asking for a friend.

My children are like inmates at a jail: They eat for free, they claim to be innocent, and they don't like the warden.

Child: The news said it's more sanitary to sneeze into an elbow. Me: They mean your own elbow!

Momageddon Academy

Homeschooling is just standing behind your kid checking their math on your phone calculator.

It's three hours into homeschooling and one student is suspended for skipping class and the other one already been expelled.

Homeschool Schedule:

- 9:00 Introduction to Toilet Flushing

- 9:15 Lab: Turning off a light switch and closing a door

- 9:30 Lecture Series: Why we don't eat food under the cushions

- 10:00 Group Project: How to stop making unnecessary noise

- 10:30 Presentation: How to close a Cheez-Its bag

- 11:00 Lecture Series: It's Not all about you

- 11:30: Covering a cough 101

- 12:30 Lecture Series: What happens when we eat all the Froot Loops in one day

- 1:00 Advanced chewing with your mouth closed

- 1:30 Lecture Series: The importance of changing underwear

- 2:00 field trip: how to have fun without leaving the porch

- 2:30 Lecture Series: reading is not punishment

- 3:00 Essay Topic: How to fill twelve hours of screen time

House rules 2: Did you go into the refrigerator at school? No. So use your school stomach.

Our homeschooling curriculum includes Honors Laundry and AP Vacuuming.

Been homeschooling a 6-year-old and an 8-year-old for one hour and 11 minutes. Teachers deserve to make a billion dollars a year. Or a week.

8-year-old is covered in paint. 17-year-old is not speaking to me because pandemic is ruining her social life and it's obviously my fault.

Feeling guilty about your kid watching too much tv? Just mute it and put the captions on. Boom. Now they're reading.

If they shut schools for too long, the mothers are going to find a solution for the virus before the scientists.

The real emergency is going to happen in 20 years when all those kids are adults, with a homeschool education brought to them by day drinking.

Dear Teachers: Send an answer key home for us parents! We're struggling with this stuff, too!

Dear Teachers,

> Next year you better make those school supply lists extravagant. You want 20 glue sticks? You got it! You want those fancy, pre-sharpened pencils by the dozens? Done. You want 12 bottles of Titos Vodka? I won't even question it. I got you, boo. Also, please let me know when it's your birthday, heck, even your momma's birthday. We are going to spoil you!

> These are my kids. And I love them. But my gosh, are they insane balls of energy that never stop eating. How do you do it?! No, seriously what's the secret?

> We miss you.

> *--Your children's other parent*

If a meeting to reopen schools takes place via ZOOM for the safety of the participants, maybe you shouldn't be discussing opening the schools. Just sayin'.

Other Family Matters and Relationship Advice

I imagine that by now a lot of husbands are ready to build that she shed.

Life status: we're currently holding it all together with one bobby pin.

Day 1 of working at home: My wife has already filed a harassment complaint with HR.

Day 2 without Sports: Found a young lady sitting on my couch yesterday. Apparently she's my wife. She seems nice.

Day 9: My wife called out from the other room and asked if I ever get a stabbing pain in my chest like someone has a voodoo doll of me and is stabbing it. I replied no. She responded, how about now?

Thank God my wife has multiple personalities. I'm quarantined with someone different every day.

Wife: Did I get fat during quarantine? Husband: You weren't really skinny to begin with! Time of death: 11:00 p.m. Cause: Covid

Some kids are starting to notice that they haven't seen their "uncle" since their Dad has been home.

Be good to your spouse. Remember, right now they could poison you and it would be counted as a Covid death.

For the second part of this quarantine, do we have to stay with the same family or are they going to relocate us? Asking for a friend.

Thoughts and prayers going out to all the husbands who've spent months telling their wives: I'll do that when I've got time.

Yesterday my husband thought he saw a cockroach in the kitchen. He sprayed everything down and cleaned thoroughly. Today I'm putting the cockroach in the bathroom.

If I'm quarantined with my wife for 2 weeks and I die... it wasn't the virus.

My wife made me coffee this morning and winked at me as she handed me the cup. I've never been more scared of a drink in all my life.

Note to wife: Hi, Darling. I'm down at the pub with my friends having a quiet drink. Unfortunately, someone just coughed so we have been quarantined. See you in 14 days!

My wife finally was able to open a jar of pickles and has declared me nonessential.

"If only we got to spend more time together." Another illusion out the window

If you're starting to feel love for your partner… don't worry, it's Stockholm Syndrome.

I have the most loving wife. Last night I woke up while she was holding a pillow tightly over my face to protect me from COVID-19.

Returned from the grocery store with the hubby. Took masks off. It turned out it was the wrong hubby! Be attentive!

Husband: I heard a symptom of the virus is no taste. Wife, looking at his shoes: you should get tested.

How long is social distancing supposed to last? My husband keeps trying to get into the house.

Him: Aw, Babe, look at you getting romantic with all of these candles. Her: First of all, I'm about to sacrifice you.

Sitting on the couch and my husband sweetly whispered… "the best part about all this is that I get to spend more time with you" as I looked over at him and lovingly realized he was talking to the dog not me.

Y'all married people holding up ok? I haven't seen "I'm so blessed" or "He's my everything" in quite a while…

I asked my husband what he's up to today and he said "none of your business". Quarantine is going well.

Ladies… check on your sisters-in-law! They are stuck at home with your brothers. They are Not OK!

After isolation:

- Where's your husband?
- In the garden.
- I don't see him.
- You need to dig a little.

Use protection during quarantine! I can't afford to come to 27 baby showers in December because y'all got bored...

Everyone keeps saying there is going to be a baby boom when this is all over. There may be a lot of divorces and justifiable homicides, too.

Eventually, everyone will be quarantined to their houses with no sports to watch. And in 9 months from now a boom of babies will be born. And we will call them the coronials.

Heard that children born 9 months from now will be called the "children of the quarn".

Prediction: There will be a minor baby boom in 9 months, and then one day in 2033, we shall witness the rise of the Quaranteens (which will be a great name for a trivia team, a rock band, a Balderdash question, or a Words with Friends entry!).

Nine months from now I better not see Ko'Rona Vyress 6 lbs. 5 oz.

I want to get quarantined with you. –Flirting in 2020

Coronavirus Pickup Lines:

- Since all the public libraries are closed, I'm checking you out instead.

- If COVID-19 doesn't take you out... Can I?

- Is that hand sanitizer in your pocket or are you just happy to be within 6 feet of me?

- You can't spell virus without U and I.

- Baby, do you need toilet paper? Because I can be your Prince Charmin.

- I saw you from across the bar. Stay there.

- Without you my life is as empty as the supermarket shelf.

- Hey, Babe! Can I ship you a drink?

- You can't spell quarantine without U R A Q T.

- Baby, it's COVID-19 outside.

Working from Home

Virtual meetings have become de rigueur during the crisis. Many of us are working, teaching or taking courses from home, attending medical appointments, and Zoom has become a noun and a verb, just ahead of Skype and Blackboard. Here are a few memes and insights from the Internet on virtual etiquette.

Boss: Why are you late? Me: Traffic, sir. Boss: But you're working online. Me: Network traffic, sir.

Not muting your mic is the new Reply All.

Sorry I'm late but I got here as soon as I wanted to.

Accidentally chose the inappropriate background for staff Zoom meeting…

Dressing for work can be so stressful. Black yoga pants, blue yoga pants, grey yoga pants?

Texting is a full-time job under quarantine and should be treated as such.

I'm out of bed and I made it to the keyboard. What more do you want?

Webinar? Oh, I'm sorry. I thought you said "wine bar".

Before you complain about your current situation, just remember: someone is quarantined with your ex.

Might sleep on the couch to cut down on my morning commute.

I love working from home. I get along with everyone at the office, I can show up in my pyjamas, and I'm always Employee of the Month.

- Disney World: Closed
- NBA: Closed
- NHL: Closed
- MLB: Closed
- My Job: See ya tomorrow.

It's amazing how badly we're screwing up an apocalypse on the "easy" setting. We're clearly not ready for zombies and aliens.

People: I want 2020 to be like the roaring 20s. Earth: Alright, infectious disease is spreading. People: No, not like that. Earth: The U.S. stock market is tanking. People: Wait. Earth: LMAO. Bars can't be open any more.

So, after this quarantine… will the producers of My 600 Pound Life just find me… or do I call them… or how will this work?

Post-it notes have become a chic home accessory.

I don't always work from home. But when I do, I don't wear pants.

Sofa: Employee of the Month parking.

If showing up in a robe and tiara with a box of wine is wrong, then maybe I don't fully understand how Casual Friday actually works.

Best thing to say if you're caught sleeping at your desk:

- They told me at the blood bank this might happen.
- The coffee machine is broken.
- Someone must have put decaf in the wrong pot.
- Why did you interrupt me? I had almost figured out a solution to our biggest problem!
- …in God's name, amen.

Pro-tip for couples suddenly working from home together: Get yourselves an imaginary co-worker to blame things on. In our apartment, Cheryl keeps leaving her dirty water cups all over the place and we really don't know what to do about her.

When you have to work from home but you're also a parent: Working 9-9:10, 9:45-10:00, 10:20-10:35, 12:30-2:00, 2:15-2:16, 3:30-3:37, 4:28-4:39, 5:05-5:12, 7:39-8:00, 9:53-10:24

Mum is in a meeting. Do not enter. The answer to your question might be here:

- Upstairs
- In the wash
- I don't know what's for dinner.
- No
- In your bedroom

- Piece of fruit

"I'm not wearing pants." 2019 — phone sex   2020 — Board Meeting

Working from home: Casual Friday Every Day.

Paranoia has reached absurd stages… I sneezed in front of my computer and the anti-virus started a scan all on its own!

Me: This show is boring. Boss: Again, this is a zoom conference.

My email saying I'll be working from home is all the work I'll be doing today.

The number one benefit of working from home: the short commute.

Work from home: destroying micromanagement by the minute.

We've decided that we'd like you to work from home, preferably for someone else.

Side effect of quarantine is it's really hard to end phone calls. Twice today I almost said "Ok, I have to run" before realizing there is nowhere to run.

Day one: I work from home. How cool! Day two: It would be nice to have someone to talk to. Day three: I hope Billy the pigeon comes to visit my window today.

Please be quiet so that mama can at least sound professional.

I wonder how many miles I've scrolled with my thumb.

No thanks, pants. I'm working from home today.

Zoom meeting dress code:

- Pajamas should not have spaghetti straps, or spaghetti on them.

- Pajamas should not have holes or inappropriate graphics — and certainly not inappropriate holes.

- Onesies must be functionally buttoned, although any attached animal heads may be worn in the up position, so long as they do not obstruct your face.

- Please do not mix story lines. Frozen and Tangled are not to be worn together.

- Same for Star Wars and Star Trek.

- Only approved Marvel/DC crossover universes may be combined. Please contact HR for guidance.

Conference Call Bingo Entries

Hi, who just joined?	Can you email that to everyone?	Is ____ on the call?	Uh, _____, you're still sharing.
Hey, guys, I have to jump to another call.	*(Sound of someone typing, possibly with a hammer)*	*(Loud, painful echo/feedback)*	*(Child or animal noises)*
Hi, can you hear me?	No, it's still loading.	Next slide, please.	Can everyone go on mute?
I'm sorry. I was on mute.	*(For overtalkers)* Sorry, go ahead.	Hello? Hello?	So *(cuts out)* I can *(unintelligible)* by *(cuts out)* OK?
Sorry I'm late *(insert lame excuse)*.	I have a hard stop at…	I'm sorry, you cut out there.	Can we take this offline?
I'll have to get back to you.	Can everyone see my screen?	Sorry, I was having connection issues.	I think there's a lag.

Who Was That Masked Man (or Woman?)

In line this morning at the Post Office, three people came in wearing masks. Panic! Then they said, "This is a robbery," and we all calmed down.

If "all lives matter", why won't you wear a mask in the grocery store?

New Queen Lyrics: No mask on your face. You big disgrace. Spreading your germs all over the place.

They said a mask and gloves were enough to go to the grocery store. They lied. Everybody else had clothes on.

If you can read this mask, you are too close!

Masks are like pants. If you're not wearing any, then you're exposing others to things that they'd rather not deal with.

Wearing a face mask is better than wearing a ventilator mask. Staying in your room is better than staying in the ICU. Washing your hands is better than washing your life away.

Praying is better than complaining right now. Stay home. Stay safe.

Walmart is now asking all customers to wear masks. Good luck with that. You can't even get them all to wear pants.

LMMO: Laughing My Mask Off

LMFMO: Laughing My Freakin' Mask Off

Remember laughing at Michael Jackson for wearing a mask and gloves? Now you're all out here looking like you wanna be starting something.

Never in my wildest dreams did I imagine I'd go up to a bank teller with a mask on asking for money.

Ripping off your mask when you get back in the car is the new taking off your bra when you get home.

Maybe some people should start using duct tape instead of a mask.

If you're driving alone in your car with a face mask on, stay home, even after this is over.

(Guy breathing a sigh of relief) Caption: When you work at a bank and two guys wearing masks come in but they're just robbing the place.

People driving alone in their cars wearing masks is the reason why there's instructions on shampoo bottles.

No shirt, no shoes, no service wasn't affecting your rights. Neither does no masks, no service.

What if we stopped thinking about masks as a sign of being controlled by the government and simply wore them to protect cashiers and others in high risk jobs as an act of kindness?

Unless you're an android, wear a mask. You might save a life.

Hannibal didn't wear a mask for his safety. He wore it for yours.

Remember "Click it or ticket"? Morons hated seatbelts, but it saved lives. Maybe we'll start "Mask it or casket" for the same reason?

Coronavirus Tip #3046. While wearing a mask, you can mouth the words "%^& you" all day long to someone's face and they will never know it.

I wear a mask because I care about protecting your life. You don't wear a mask because...

If you hate wearing a mask, you're really not going to like the ventilator.

Why you should wear face masks. Let me make this simple: The Urine Test.

- If we all run around naked and someone pees on you, you get wet right away.

- If you are wearing pants, some pee will get through, but not as much, so you are better protected.

- If the guy who pees also is wearing pants, the pee stays with him and you do not get wet.

I know masks aren't exactly comfortable, but neither are bras, and a good portion of the population wears those regularly for far less important reasons.

If you all don't start wearing masks then you are going to have to homeschool your kids this fall. Hope this helps.

A mask is not a political statement. It is an IQ test.

Lol. Seeing guys that spent the last twenty years prepping their bunker to survive indefinitely in a nuclear winter are giving up after wearing a thin cloth mask for three weeks.

The Reopening

So is coronavirus over, or is this the halftime show?

Congratulations. You have successfully made it to the end of May. Welcome to Level 6 of Jumanji.

The seven dwarves have been told that from Monday, they can meet in groups of six. One of them isn't Happy.

I'm going to put the Jumanji board away now, guys. Sorry for the inconvenience.

Here's a very appropriate analogy: "The curve is flattening; we can start lifting restrictions now." = "The parachute has slowed our rate of descent; we can take it off now."

How many of you believe that this is ending in 2 weeks and your life is back to normal? Raise your hand. Now slap yourself with it.

I don't always go to Georgia during a pandemic, but when I do, I go bowling and get a tattoo.

At the store was an X on the floor by the register for me to stand. I've seen too many Road Runner cartoons to fall for that.

Like a good neighbor, stay over there.

I'm pretty sure "put yourself on mute" is going to be a popular phrase when classrooms reopen.

Fact: For everyone saying America won't reopen, remember Jurassic Park opened 5 times after people were eaten alive. Five.

If someone told you a roller coaster was almost fixed, would you get on it? Please stay home!

Be like this little piggy (stayed home)

When quarantine is over, let's not tell some people.

The whole country could be tested by midnight if they'd let the Chick-fil-A crew run the drive-through testing sites.

If graduation can't be done inside a gym or outside on a football field, perhaps the grads could walk through Walmart, Lowe's or Home Depot and be announced over the speaker.

Remember the mayor in "Jaws" was so concerned about the economy, he told everyone it was safe to go back in the water? Just saying

The check you're getting is to stimulate the American economy, not China, so buy American and shop small businesses.

Just because the server walked to your car instead of your table, doesn't mean you don't have to tip. Now is not the time to be that kind of person. Make sure you tip when you order to go.

If you are out protesting to open the state, please stay out of the hospital when you get sick. Treat yourself since you know what's best.

We're allowed back to work, but you've got to remember:

- Avoid MEN
  - M mouth
  - E eyes
  - N nose

- Instead, follow WOMEN
  - W wash your hands
  - O obey social distancing
  - M mask up
  - E exercise and eat well
  - N no unnecessary traveling

Commercials in 2030 will include: Were you or someone you know overly exposed to hand sanitizer, Lysol, or bleach during the 2020 coronavirus pandemic? If so, you may be eligible for compensation.

When all this is over, please continue to stay at least six feet away from me at all times.

Soon-to-be-popular tee-shirts:

- Straight Outta Quarantine.

- I survived the Great Toilet Paper Shortage of 2020.

- Quarantine Vegan: I Avoid Meet.

- Take the Panic out of Pandemic.

- Staying Away from Positive People #2020

- I was social distancing before it was cool.

- If you can read this shirt you are too close. Please step back.

- I wear a mask to protect you. Please return the favor.

- I have a mask and you have an automatic weapon. Whose grandmother is safer?

If we're going to have one-way aisles in the grocery stores, then I'm going to need a passing lane.

Social distancing is going pretty well so far. Found some great reading material at the cabin, so I'm set for a bit.

What you do you to bet those murder hornets are going to be attracted to hand sanitizer?

Can't see bras coming back after this.

When scheduling reopening, remember: the early worm gets eaten.

Fewer graves if we reopen in waves.

Noah didn't go swimming in the flood to prove his faith in God. He showed his faith by staying in the ark and waiting until it was safe to come out.

When this is all over, we are throwing the biggest St. Patrick's Easter de Mayo of July party anyone's ever seen.

Once they come out with a corona virus vaccine, I don't want to see any of you antivaxxers getting one. Don't be a hypocrite!

Nothing should go back to normal. Normal wasn't working.

The spread of COVID-19 is based upon two factors. 1. How dense the population is. 2. How dense the population is.

You were never told to surrender your civil liberties. You were asked to help each other stay healthy and survive.

Since hockey has been cancelled, no one has seen the Zamboni Driver. But I'm sure he will resurface eventually.

News story: Man arrested for putting down fake social distancing arrows in Ikea and creating a labyrinth with no exit.

Swimming pools will reopen on the 4th of July. Due to continuing Social Distancing rules, there will be no water in lanes 1, 3, and 5.

Dear July, I don't want any trouble from you. Just come in, sit down, don't touch anything, and keep your mouth shut.

Random Words of Wisdom

Alien 1: Hey, Whatchya up to? Alien 2: Watching Season 2020 of Earth. Stuff's getting' wild!

What kind of jokes does the CDC recommend now? Inside jokes.

One cough a day, keeps all humans away.

Time Magazine Person of the Year 2020: Mayhem

When the Covid-19 horror is over and we go back to our normal lives, never forget that during the crisis we were not desperate for lawyers, actors, athletes, or reality tv stars. We needed teachers, doctors, nurses, shop workers, delivery drivers, and countless others whom we usually take for granted.

Time to re-watch "Monk", but this time take notes!

If I've learned one thing from this coronavirus outbreak, from now on, I'm going to stop eating bats.

2020 Bingo entries, including:

Queen of England dies	"Cats: The Butthole Version" released	Sharks with Laser Beams	Naked Donald Trump Picture Leaked
Jesus Returns	Alien Invasion	World Wide Power Outage	Coronavirus mutates
Civil War	New Make-Up Trend: Unibrows	Ghosts are proven to be real	Volcano erupts at Yellowstone
Godzilla	Rats of unusual size	Firefly season two, but it's awful	Animal crossing hacked—all progress erased
Meteor hits Earth	Second stimulus check but it's just a $20 gift card to Applebees	Giant Murder Hornets	Super gonorrhea outbreak
Fog that turns you inside out	Disney World alligator infestation	North Korea nuclear threat	Brown recluse spiders evolve wings

Back to the Future Rule Number One: Never set it to 2020.

2020 every second: But wait, there's more.

Years from now we're gonna be like 2018, 2019, 2021, 2022. "Hey, you missed…" "Nope! We don't talk about that one!"

Your grandparents were called to war. You're being called to sit on your couch. You can do this.

(Captain Kirk sitting at a table with a sign): 2020 is the Kobayashi Maru. Change my mind.

I know this. When it ends, and it will, every restaurant will have a 2-hour wait, every kid will be glad to be in school, everyone will love their job, the stock market will skyrocket, every other house will get TP'd, and we'll all embrace and shake hands. That's gonna be a pretty good day. Hang in there, World.

Snow White is down to six dwarfs. Sneezy has been placed into quarantine.

Wanna keep these Millennials home in Quarantine? Simple. Replace their transmission with a stick shift and print the manual in Cursive.

All of a sudden, everybody has become Sheldon.

Can we uninstall 2020 and install it again? This version has a virus.

Did you hear that the Spanish king has been quarantined on his private jet? This means that the reign in Spain will stay mainly in the plane.

The English are feeling the pinch and have raised their virus threat level from "miffed" to "peeved". Soon, though, the level may be raised again to "irritated" or even "a bit cross".

T-Rex: Couldn't wash hands. Is now extinct.

Dr. Crusher would have cured COVID-19 and still have 10 minutes left in this terrible episode.

As long as we don't see apes on horseback with guns... we're still doing ok.

Keep calm. It's just my allergies.

Whoever said one person can't change the world never ate an undercooked bat.

Sign at some kind of protest: Every disaster movie starts with the government ignoring a scientist.

Now would be the perfect time for Walmart to take all of its carts and get a wheel alignment done on them.

Wesley: Why aren't there handles on doors anymore? Picard: Wesley, it's time I tell you about the year 2020...

Has anyone tried playing curling (I should stop there, but let's keep going) with a Roomba? Those dust bunnies are excellent things you can sweep to try to slow it down or change course.

We've reached introvert nirvana. All events canceled, we don't have to talk sports. No one is making physical contact or random small talk.

Wash your hands like you're washing Jason Momoa.

Breaking News: John Travolta was suspected of having COVID-19. Doctors now confirm that it was only Saturday Night Fever, and they assure us that he is Staying Alive.

Coronavirus, fires in Australia, trillions of locusts in Kenya, earthquakes in Puerto Rico, murder wasps killing bees. Did we miss the memo on where to show up for the Rapture?

I think the world is going to owe a big apology to Detective Monk.

For the love of God, do all of the road construction now!

Corona virus pandemic, daylight savings time, Friday the 13th and a full moon all in the same week… Who out there is playing Jumanji?

So there was a time change this week, a full moon, it's Friday the 13th and the coronavirus is spreading. Can the person who is playing Jumanji please stop before Jason and Freddy Krueger show up? Real life is becoming stranger than fiction.

Congratulations! You've successfully made it to April. Welcome to Level 4 of Jumanji.

This too shall pass. It might pass like a kidney stone, but it shall pass.

Wash your hands like you just ate crawfish and you need to take your contacts out.

Wash your hands like you just got done slicing jalapenos for a bunch of nachos and you need to take your contacts out.

2020 is a unique leap year. It has 29 days in February, 300 days in March, and 5 years in April.

Marijuana is legal. Haircuts are not. It took 50 years, but the hippies have finally won.

What COVID-19 has taught us: Half of our jobs can be done at home. The other half deserve more than they're being paid.

Don't believe everything you read on the Internet about Covid-19. Bob Dylan, Drummer, Metallica

Just sneezed in my mask. How's your morning going?

Because of Covid for the first time the National Spelling Bee is cancil… cancul… cansel… It's been called off.

Never travel with Tom Hanks. His ship got hijacked. His plane crashed. He got stuck at an airport. He was stranded on an island. And now has COVID-19.

Due to the short supply of disinfectants and cleaning supplies, dirty deeds will no longer be done dirt cheap.

Louisiana now has a new parish. It's called Bayou Self.

Has anyone checked on the Yellowstone super volcano? Or is that next month's episode?

Who had Yellowstone supervolcano for June?

Just a warning. Next week starts with changing the clocks, moves to a full moon and ends with a Friday the 13th. Good luck people! PS: Don't forget to wash your hands.

Best Realtor one-liner of the day: Can you see yourself quarantined here?

When you sneeze in your house and everyone yells "corona" rather than "bless you".

CDC recommends washing your hands for 20 seconds. You know what takes roughly 20 seconds to say? "Space. The Final Frontier. These are the voyages of the starship Enterprise. Its continuing mission: to explore strange new worlds. To seek out new life and new civilizations. To boldly go where no one has gone before." You're not required to hum the theme afterwards, but who's gonna stop you, honestly.

2020 Calendar:

- January – Australia is on fire.

- February – Kobe dies.

- March – COVID 19 is coming to kill us.

- April – Economy tanks; UFOs are real.

- May – Giant murder hornets <- You are here.

- June – Underground crab people are discovered and they eat humans.

- July – Apes with guns on horseback come for the human race.

- August – Godzilla comes out of the ocean and he's angry.

- September – Zombie outbreak as a result of the COVID 19 vaccine testing.

- October - My Little Pony turns out to be real and they eat humans, also.

- November – Second wave of crab people.

- December – Cthulhu comes out of the ocean and he's angry.

- January 2021 – Aliens invade planet earth.

- February 2021 – Cleveland Browns win the Super Bowl.

- March 2021 – Rapture

- April 2021 – Avengers 5 comes out.

Chuck Norris was exposed to the coronavirus. The virus is now in quarantine for 2 weeks.

Me: I think I'm ready to date again. The Universe: Oh yeah? (releases world-wide virus that prevents human interaction) Me: Well played.

Due to coronavirus we are self-isolating. No one may enter except:
- Keanu Reeves
- Matthew McConaughey
- George Clooney
- And those firefighter guys holding puppies who we saw on a calendar.

Remember when you wished the weekend would last forever? You happy now?

My farmer friend used his stimulus check to buy baby chickens. He got money for nothing and his chicks for free.

For the love of God wash your hands and turn off the news.

They say you can't fix stupid. Turns out you can't quarantine it, either.

"Social distancing" is boring. "Exiled for the good of the realm" sounds much more interesting.

2020 is a unique leap year. It has 29 days in February, 180 days in March, 9 months in April, and so far we're 6 years into May.

Of all the stupid things I've done in life, if I die because I touched my face I'm going to be ticked.

And just like that, Adrian Monk's behavior is normal.

T-Rex: I'll survive. I can't touch my face.

Giant Meteor 2020. Just end it already.

Keep complaining about the quarantine. You just bought yourself another month. You wanna keep going, pal? I can do this all 2020.

Star Trek: No Contact. Social distancing is not futile.

So how's 2020? Oh, there was a virus outbreak. And Kobe Bryant died. And Australia was on fire. But the memes are great.

This is the longest something Made in China has ever lasted.

Breaking News: A Plant has been discovered to cure the coronavirus… Plant yo butt on that couch and don't leave the house.

What happens in quarantine stays in quarantine.

Where is Morgan Freeman? Shouldn't he be narrating this or something?

Be like Darth Vader.

- Wears a mask.
- Doesn't visit his son and daughter.
- Socially and emotionally distant.
- Follows orders.

Abbott: So, they're saying that coronavirus is now officially a pandemic.

Costello: Who says?

Abbott: Yes.

Costello: Who did?

Abbott: Of course, that's their job.

Costello: Whose job?

Abbott: Exactly.

Costello: And what is the name of that organization?

Abbott: Not what… WHO.

Costello: That's what I'm trying to find out!

World: There's no way we can shut down everything in order to lower emissions, slow climate change and protect the environment. Mother Nature: Here's a virus. Practice.

Covidiot, noun co-vid-i-ot kou-'vi-di-at

- A stupid person who stubbornly ignores "social distancing" protocol, thus helping to further spread Covid-19. "Are you seriously going to visit grandma? Dude, don't be such a covidiot."

- A stupid person who hoards groceries, needlessly spreading Covid-19 fears and depriving others of vital supplies. "See that guy with the 200 toilet paper rolls? What a covidiot."

2020 Canceled:

After careful consideration, we have decided that it is no longer in the best interests of everyone involved to proceed with 2020.

While we recognize that a lot of hard work has gone into preparing for 2020, if we're honest, it has turned into a bit of a $%^&* and we feel it is best to just call it off.

We understand that some of you were looking forward to seeing what cruel and peculiar)(*&^% of a disaster 2020 would throw up next. But on balance we believe it is probably best not to find out.

We will instead provide ticket-holders with a full refund or an exchange, and start afresh with 2021 on Monday.

Our plan is to deliver a more enjoyable year, similar to say 2016, which everyone thought was the absolute worst year of all time, but in retrospect was a ^&*@# walk in the park.

See you next year.

--Management

Imagine surviving Covid-19 and then China releases Covid-19S Plus Pro.

OK, but honestly, how blessed are we that during a global pandemic, we can just stay warm at home, reading, working, still being educated, creating, talking to our loved ones, with little worries and a fridge stocked with food? Do remind yourself to be grateful today.

Library sign: Please note: The post-apocalyptical fiction section has been moved to Current Affairs.

PSA: Not everyone that coughs or sneezes is carrying your big scary virus. Some of us have seasonal allergies and don't appreciate your death glares.

In the year 2020 humanity was threatened with extinction. Panic spread across the planet like never before. What were you doing, Grandpa? Just sending memes to friends and stuff.

People are asking me, "Is Covid-19 Really that serious?" Listen, y'all, the casinos and churches are closed. When Heaven and Hell Agree on the same thing, it's probably pretty serious.

Coronavirus memes are spreading faster than the coronavirus.

If you don't say Covid-19 to the tune of "Come on Eileen," you do now. You're welcome.

Well, That Didn't Work: A Brief History of 2020

2020 is gonna be a symbol for "crazy" for the rest of time:

- "yo, my man over there is a little…you know…2020.

- "I gained control of the car for a moment, your honor, and then things went 2020."

If you could end coronavirus by sacrificing one genre of music, what would it be and why country music?

Coronavirus explained in craft terms: You and 9 friends are crafting. 1 is using glitter. How many projects have glitter?

WANDERING
WOODS
PUBLISHERS

Other Wandering Woods Publishers titles by Ed Mickolus

His Words

Take My Weight… Please! (with Joe Rendon)

Two Spies Walk Into a Bar

The Secret Book of CIA Humor

The Secret Book of Intelligence Community Humor

Terrorism Worldwide 2019

Spycraft for Thriller Writers

About the author: Edward Mickolus snuck off with a Ph.D. from Yale University before they noticed it was missing. He was a CIA analyst, operations officer and manager for 33 years. He taught writing, briefing, creativity and other techniques at the CIA, the FBI Academy and other federal agencies. He runs Vinyard Software, Inc., and has authored 40 books (collect them all!), including *The Secret Book of CIA Humor.* He is a recovering standup comic.

CPSIA information can be obtained
at www.ICGtesting.com
Printed in the USA
BVHW070718201120
593719BV00012B/872